Purposed On Purpose

Purposed On Purpose

Janice Buckley

Purposed on Purpose

J. Kenkade Publishing
6104 Forbing Rd
Little Rock, AR 72209
www.jkenkadepublishing.com
Facebook.com/jkenkadepublishing

J. Kenkade Publishing is a registered trademark.

Printed in the United States of America
ISBN 978-1-955186-03-2

Table of Contents

Introduction: Broken But Healed

I was broken. I felt lost. I was afraid. I had anxiety. I was in doubt. I didn't believe. Little did I know, all I had to do was believe I was healed, and that would give me access to healing. I am not trying to throw a pity party, but when I look back over that timeframe, I was choosing to rest in brokenness. I was choosing to sit in a place where I felt alone, knowing that I had access to God, so I had to put myself to the side in order for me to see and hear God. To be honest, it was God who got me through the times where I couldn't see my way out of this situation. I was about to give up on love because I thought that there wasn't anyone in this world who could love me for me, and I was about to give up on purpose because I didn't see myself the way that God sees me. God had to remind me of who I was in Him. God gave me a glimpse of what my Purpose was in Him and what it was going to take for me to start walking in my Purpose. Have you ever been in a dark place in life and no matter where you turned, you felt like no one was in your corner? That's where I was in this season. Little did I know,

God was preparing me for times that would require me to have faith in moments of adversity.

Faith requires you to believe the impossible, to see things for the good even when they look bad, to believe God no matter what the circumstances look like, and to stand firm when fear tries to scare you into unbelief. For a moment, I felt like Job because it seemed like everything kept coming left and right, but I never lost hope, and I never stopped believing God. In the book of Job, the devil asks for permission from God to bother Job. God had confidence in Job that he would not curse God or betray God, no matter what happened in his life. Job had lost his children, and he was losing everything around him; even his health was threatened. Job kept his faith in God and never turned on God. This book is actually a journey about how my faith was tested and how I overcame my fears, which led me right into the arms of Purpose. God purposed me on Purpose to do the work in the Earth for His Kingdom, for the building up, and for leading people back to Christ, who is the way, the truth, and the life. The ways of Christ lead us, the truths of Christ set us free, and His life gives us hope and new beginnings.

God will set you up with the right person at the right time and create the opportunity for you to walk in Purpose. I learned a long time ago that if what I'm doing does not serve my Purpose, then why am I doing it? Your Purpose and the person who God has for you will line up with what God is trying to do in your life, not for your own needs and wants but to serve and meet the needs of others. Your assignment is way bigger than you, and you may not understand why you are supposed to be doing certain things, but when you see the lives of the people connected to you flourish, then that's when you know that your works are from God and for serving His people. I would always ask God to allow me to be a blessing to someone and allow me to be used to serve someone or bless them. When I think about this, what am I getting from this? I don't benefit from this, but the beautiful thing about this is that I'm not looking to get anything from it because the heart of God lives on the inside of me, so I truly want to see all of God's children blessed and prospering. No, I cannot be their savior, but what I can do is lead them to the same One who saved my life, who pulled me out of those dark places when I didn't see a way out.

It was all *God*!

I am here to tell you that God will never leave you nor forsake you, but He will lift you up above any circumstance that tries to hold you bound. God will set you free in your mind, body, and spirt. If He did it for me, then He definitely can do the same thing for you.

Chapter 1

†

Purposed with Manifestations

"In the beginning was the Word, and the Word was with God, and the Word was God"
John 1:1

This is a Bible verse, right? But I also want to genuinely encourage you by letting you know that. God will speak a word to you to reveal your Purpose, your calling, and your work in the Earth for His Kingdom. You will not have to second-guess it; it will resonate in your spirit. It is wisdom.

A lot of the time, people say that they do not hear from God or they ask, "How do you hear from God?" God speaks to us daily, and it does not have to always be in word. Sometimes, it could be in a dream or vision, and it may even be through someone close to you because God has His ways to get to you. Any time I want to reach out to God, I am always reminded of the scripture, "But seek ye first the kingdom of God, and his righteousness; and all things things shall be added unto you" (Matthew 6:33). I use this scripture as a source of strength, and the words speak to my spirit and give me reassurance in knowing that God has my best interest at heart. When I seek Him, He will meet me right where I am and give me knowledge and understanding. Knowing who you are (and Whose you are) makes a big difference when seeking your Purpose. God will reveal to you what you need to be doing for His Kingdom, and when you find yourself is when you find your Purpose. Finding your Purpose is not a coincidence. In fact, God's purpose for you was predestined way before the foundations of the Earth and before He even formed you in your mother's womb.

"But you are a chosen generation, a royal priesthood, a holy nation, His own special people, that you may proclaim the praises of Him who called you out of darkness into His marvelous light..."
(1 Peter 2:9, NKJV)

We walk in the light of God. We are His people who are set apart to do His will. Your Purpose is defined in you knowing who you are!

Do not forget where you come from, or you will be confused about where you are going.

You are destined for greatness! The path God has set out for you is inevitable. The things that God has for you to do is intentional and for His glory. Are you seeking God for your Purpose and for His will for your life? This answer may take time, and I am here to tell you that it will not come overnight. We all want this "microwave" lifestyle (we want everything quickly), not realizing how much more that harms us than helps us. I do not know about you, but when I want a good meal – I'm talking about a meal good for my soul – I don't want it quickly. I want it slow-cooked and made with love. For your Purpose to begin unfolding in your life, you must seek God, for He is the creator of all things, He is all-knowing, and He is omnipotent! Matthew 6: 33 says, "But seek ye first the kingdom of God; and his righteousness; and all these things shall be added unto you." That scripture alone speaks volumes.

I rose early one morning. The sun was shining through my room, and I spoke out loud, "Lord, I rise early, and I seek You. I seek you with my whole heart. I seek you with determination, knowing you have something just for me!" When you pray and seek God, He will reveal to you His heart. He will show you the way He sees you through His eyes. You will know this when you begin to see yourself as being great and as more than a conqueror. When God's words begin to resonate with you, what anyone else has to say about you becomes irrelevant. I do not know about you, but I want God's best and nothing less! Before you and I even existed, the Lord formed us in our mother's wombs. He knew us before He formed the world! God knows what is best for us, and He knows our beginnings before our ends. We are His workmanship. We are His masterpiece!

His Word declares, "For I know the plans I have for you...plans to prosper you and not to harm you, plans to give you hope and a future." (Jeremiah 29:11, NIV)

"...Decree a thing, and it shall be established..." (Job 22:28)

Speaking life into a dead situation may seem unbelievable– yes, I know. Experience became a great teacher as I was going through a trial in my life, not knowing how great of a testimony it was growing to be. I had just found out I was pregnant, and I was excited to share the news with family. Well, about two weeks later, I was headed to the doctor's office to hear the baby's heartbeat. The ultrasound tech came in, and she put the cold jelly on my stomach and began moving the ultrasound instrument around my belly, looking for the baby. She stopped. She was frowning, and I asked her if something was wrong. She looked at me and told me that I would have to talk to the doctor. As she led us to his office, I was confused because she would not tell me anything. A few minutes passed, and the doctor walked in. He sat down slowly and began to tell us that the tech did not see a heartbeat on the ultrasound. At that moment, my heart dropped, and I was immediately in disbelief.

Have you ever had a piece of hope in your hands, only for it to be snatched away from you? That is exactly how I felt. I was hurt! I thought about all the things that I could have done wrong to cause this.

I asked the doctor what it was that I did to cause this.

His response was, "Nothing, sometimes things like this happen."

I thought to myself, *Why me*?

As I was leaving the doctor's office, I was in denial. I started hoping that maybe I was not as far along as I thought and that if I waited a few more weeks, we would find a heartbeat. Well, I was wrong because about three days later, I began having a miscarriage. Shortly after the miscarriage, I began to heal spiritually because after that experience I felt broken, I felt lost, and I was confused. So, I started to seek God for clarity. I needed a solution! I was watching a video of Sara Jakes Roberts, and she was teaching on the woman with the issue of blood. She caught my attention because that is one of my favorite faith stories in the Bible. If you do not know about the woman with the issue of blood, well, she was determined to be healed, and she was not going to let anything or anyone stop her. She had been been dealing with this for twelve years. She heard about Jesus and how He was performing healing miracles, and she was determined to just get a touch so that she would be healed. As Jesus was moving through the crowd of people, she saw her opportunity to touch Him.

When she did, He asked, "Who touched me?"

Because of her faith, when she touched Jesus, healing immediately overcame her and made her whole. After watching the video that same day, I began speaking over my life. Daily, I would speak affirmations of healing over my body. I would declare that my womb was made whole and that no weapon formed against me would prosper! The next thing I decreed was that my womb would carry a healthy baby again to full term. I prayed that my baby would be full of wisdom and that my child would be blessed. My former husband and I started to try again, and a few months later, we found out we were having a baby. Let's just say nine months later, we had a baby boy. I'm not boasting in anything that I did but instead sharing how God manifested in my life. I had to learn to put my trust in God fully. I truly believe that when you begin walking in faith, God will show you a glimpse of what it looks like so that you will build your trust up in Him. This is a faith walk. Faith comes by hearing, and hearing comes by the Word of God. By Faith, God created the Earth and every living thing. He breathed breath into the body and gave life to a void situation. What is it that you are believing for? Start by putting your trust in God.

God is With You

God will never leave you nor will He forsake you (Hebrews 13:5, NIV). This is a scripture I learned oh-so well. I was going through a dry season in my life. I felt alone, and I felt like I didn't have anyone to talk to. I didn't have anyone to call or anyone to listen to me talk about how I felt. I remember calling on my best friend, who would always answer the phone when I called, and on this day she didn't answer. I reached out to my sister, and she didn't answer. So, then I called on my mom, and she didn't pick up either. At that point, I began to cry because I felt like I didn't have one person to call upon. I walked outside, sat on my back porch, and looked up. The sky was blue, and I began thanking God for the beautiful day.

The next thing I knew, a white dove flew down to where I was, and it got really close to me. The dove was so close that I was able to take a picture with my phone, and to this day, I have this picture. For a second, I was confused because I was trying to figure out where in the world this white dove came from. White doves represent the Holy Spirit. They represent peace. At that moment, peace surrounded me, and I didn't feel alone. I knew then that no matter where I am in life, God is always with me.

Chapter 2

†

Your Testimony Is Somebody's Breakthrough

"Those who know your name will put their trust in you, for you, Lord, have never forsaken those who seek you."
Psalm 9:10

For everything that we go through, there is a time and a season. Have you ever been afraid of sharing your testimony because you thought someone would judge you or talk about you or just out of fear? I am sure we have all been there, but I am going to share my experience with you. After having a miscarriage, yes, I was embarrassed. I did not really want to tell anyone about my pain and sadness. Eventually, I had to realize that this was never about me and that I was being a little selfish. I realized that someone needed to hear my testimony. My testimony was somebody's breakthrough! There was a couple at my church who had a miscarriage, and the woman went up for prayer. When service was over, God spoke to me and told me to ask her if I could pray for her. I was nervous at first because I did not know how she would respond to me.

But out of obedience, I asked her, anyway.

She said, "Yes, you can pray for me."

I began to pray for her!

After I did, I shared with her my experience from my miscarriage and how I would speak over my body. I told her how I would get up in the morning, and the first thing I would say was, "Thank you, Lord, for healing my body, for making my body whole, and that no weapon formed against me shall prosper!" I also prayed over my baby in the spirit, that my baby would carry out to full term, that he would be made whole and healthy, and that fear would not enter my mind. I told her to do this daily until she saw the manifestation! A few months passed, and she came to church and announced that they were expecting a baby. Now, I did not share this to brag about me, but I share this because of the work of God! Her faith in God healed her womb, and she is now a mother! God gets the glory! I honestly believe we are put here on this Earth to help each other. Often, we wonder why we must go through things. One thing is for sure– I learned that I could no longer be selfish. Out of obedience, someone was healed. The beautiful thing about helping one another is that while we share our testimonies and experiences, we are also on journeys, going through the process of building our faith in God. The goals are winning souls and leading people back to God! John 12:32 (NKJV) says, "And I, if I am lifted up from the earth, will draw all peoples to Myself."

God has already created the path for you; He is just waiting on you to walk in it.

Walk in Healing

"By His stripes, I am healed!"
Isaiah 53:5 (NKJV)

I still remember this day like it was yesterday. In October 2019, I went in to the doctor because I wasn't feeling well. I had a cough that took my voice away. I was sitting in the room, waiting on the doctor to come in, and I began to speak healing over my body. The doctor finally came in, and I explained how my throat felt and how I sounded hoarse. She took her light and looked at the back of my throat, looking concerned.

She asked me if I smoked, and I said, "No, ma'am."

She said, "Well, there is a bump on your uvula, and I'm concerned that it is cancer-related.

I said, "Oh no, not me!"

She referred me to a ear, nose and throat specialist, and it was scheduled three months out. In those three months of waiting, I decreed healing over my body and kept it between me and God only, although it was hard to keep it to myself because I tell my sisters and mom everything. This time was necessary. I had to remain silent. I was reminded of the scripture, "He who guards his mouth preserves his life..." (Proverbs 13:3, NKJV). Some things need to be kept between you and God until He says to speak on it. Three months later, I went to see the specialist, and he took a biopsy of the bump to test it for cancer. I was praying so hard during that time. One thing I can say is that during the period of waiting, I was never in fear. I was never given over to fear. Instead, God gave me a sound mind, and I was focused on healing. My test results came back, and the biopsy was benign (no cancer). I thank God for healing my body and making me whole. Truth be told, if I would have given myself over to fear, there is no telling where I would be. God is a Provider; He takes care of me. The whole time, my eyes stayed focused on God and His plan for me to live and not die, to be made whole with a body that has no sickness. I am in awe of His goodness and favor over my life, and I will forever praise Him.

Do you know what is amazing? The fact that God is no Respecter of persons, and He can do it for you, too! You are made whole, and you walk in healing, as well. Healing belongs to you, and all you have to do is believe it. I used to be afraid of how others would view me for believing in something that seemed out-of-this-world impossible. But now after experiencing healing power in my life, I'm willing to do what I have to do to walk in healing. I don't care how I look or what anyone says. I am trusting what the Word of God says. I am out here living on a word, a prayer, and and plan, and knowing what God has for me is for me. Therefore, healing belongs to me, so when I open my mouth and declare healing over my life and my circumstances. I will be healed, whole, and set free. Not one person can stop you from walking in healing. You have got to allow faith to step in and be the catalyst that leads you to your healing. Sometimes, we are our own distractions because we allow doubt, fear, and disappointments to drive our beliefs. Today is the last day for that. You have to move out of your own way and be set free! God wants the very best for you, and He no longer wants you to be bound in your mindset. God will give you provision! He will give you all the tools necessary to walk in freedom in Him.

Decree: "Lord, Your desires over my desires. Your will over my will!"

A lot of the time, we try to take control, and God is telling us to "be still" because He is God all by Himself. He does not need our help being God. We worry our little minds over nothing, and the whole time, He is working things out in our favor. We have to trust God with our whole hearts and let Him have His way.

Chapter 3

†

Purposed with Dreams

God purposed you to do the work in the Earth for His Kingdom through dreams and visions backed up with manifestations. God will give you dreams to warn you, guide you, and give you insight. He will give you visions so that you can see things supernaturally.

I remember when God gave me my first dream! I had so many questions, especially because I would see the dream manifest days later. So, I started to write down my dreams and put date on each entry. My first dream was about one of my close friends. In my dream, my close friend called me and told me that she needed to meet with me in person because she had something to tell me and she wanted to tell me in person. We met at our usual lunch spot, and she told me that she was pregnant. The very next day, my dream became reality, and everything manifested exactly the same way. In that dream, God was trying to get my attention to let me know that He gave me the gift of dreams. A few months later, I had another dream about a situation where there was chaos breaking loose and everyone was panicking. The next day, I was in class, and one of my classmates had a seizure, and no one knew what to do. All I remember doing was praying over her, and she stopped seizing before the ambulance showed up. That dream was another sign of my gift of dreams and God warning me. After these two dreams, I started to read the book of Daniel. Daniel was a dreamer, and God warned him in his dreams, too. I am sure you have had dreams and wondered what they meant or if God was trying to tell you something. The next time you have a dream, I challenge you to start writing them down in a journal. When you go back to read your journal, recap over the dream and see how it was reflected at some point in your life.

My most recent dream was about a sound. I remember waking up, and all I could hear was the sound. I just kept repeating it to myself. I thought about it, and it came to me. When you hear a sound, it gets your attention. God was telling me to change what my attention was on. The next night, I had another dream. In this one, I was cooking on the stovetop, and then there was a loud boom. The next day, I got up, and God really had my attention because at that point I felt like He was trying to tell me something. I turned on a video of Bishop T.D. Jakes, and the first thing he said was when you are experiencing the power of God in your life, you will hear a boom! The boom is a Kingdom sound, which precedes the move of God, which happens when you find deliverance and healing. I was battling with holding on to past traumas that happened in my life, and I had an issue with forgiving. God put it on my heart to go to church, and when I got there, I felt God tell me to walk around like I was free. At first, I was wondering why I needed to walk around like I was free. Well, church was almost over, and the pastor asked me to come up for prayer. When she got in front of me, she told me that I was in the spotlight the moment I walked in the door.

She said, "You need to let go of trauma right now because God is trying to use you, but you need to be set free!"

All I could do was fall down and worship God. I left church that Sunday, and I decided to start walking in freedom. I was no longer going to hold on to something that was holding me back from my Purpose. I am here to tell you that if God did it for me, then He can do it for you. Let go and let Him do the good works inside of you. You are set free in your spirit from all the things that try to hold you bound.

God Will Give You Visions

When God gives you the gift of visions, He is giving you dreams that speak to you, and they usually become reality. They are like dreams but with deeper meaning because they feel so real. Trust me, you will know. It feels like second nature. “God has given each of you a gift from his great variety of spiritual gifts. Use them to serve one another” (1 Peter 4:10, NLT). The gifts that God gives us are not only for our greater good but for the good of others. Someone in this world needs what you have.

There was a point in my life where I questioned my dreams and God revealed to me that this was not about me. This was about the mother who was carrying the load alone, the husband who didn’t feel like he was enough, the little girl who felt like she didn’t fit in, and the little boy who fought with his identity. God wants us to lead people back to Him so He gets the glory! We have to learn to be selfless. The work that God created us to do in this Earth will require our obedience to God! That is why it is vital to write down your dreams and visions and to stay in the Word of God so that He can reveal to you your Purpose.

A good prayer to pray that helps me is: "Lord, show me Your way, Your will for me, and what it is that You would have for me to do for You. Guide me on the path that You have purposed for me so I can become the person that You created me to be. In Jesus' mighty name. Amen."

You do not have to use my prayer. I am just sharing what helps me. You can allow God to lead you and give you whatever it is you need in prayer. I just want to encourage you to seek Him when it comes to walking in Purpose. You have so much greatness inside of you just waiting to get out! God does not give us visions without a purpose. Every vision that God gives us leads to a revelation. Have you ever wondered, Who am I?, or What is it that I'm supposed to be doing? Every day that you wake up is a daily reminder that you are here on Purpose. God purposed you to be the inspiration that someone needs. He chose you to be the change in someone's life. You have a gift waiting to be revealed. I was chosen to walk in Purpose, and so were you. You had better act like it! Seeking God for my Purpose brought so much light into my life as God began revealing to me in visions and dreams how my life should be so that I would not take anything less than His promises for me.

Have you ever felt refreshed, as if you were new? That was the feeling that came over me when I started realizing my Purpose. I would ask God to give me dreams, and He did. I asked God to give me visions, and He allowed me to see things before they manifested. No, I'm not perfect, and God didn't create me any different from you. We all can gain access to Purpose by seeking God. "Ask...[and] ye shall receive" (Matthew 7:7). I'm not talking about money or materialistic things. I'm talking about wisdom, insight, and understanding. Those are the keys to gaining access to Purpose. Someone once told me that I have all the keys (knowledge) that I need to do what God has called me to do. When I first heard that, I was still trying to figure out what those keys were. Now that I know what they are, I've been operating with those keys (knowledge).

God is the Source of my Strength and the Strength of My Life

How would I have known how to navigate in this world and to have access to the good things that God wants for me if I had not have sought God? Without God, I am nothing and have nothing. I would be so lost without Him. I can only imagine that living life on this Earth without God would be like going to a foreign country, walking around and trying to get from point A to point B without any navigation or guidance, not being able to speak the same language as the people in my area. How could I understand them? What a huge struggle that would be. Every single day of my life and with every breath that I take, I know without a doubt that I need the Lord.

I'm going to get a little personal with you for a moment. I was in a marriage for six years. Yes, that is a long time; I think so, anyway. Well, my ex-husband and I really didn't take the time to get to know one another. We met at work, we became friends, both of us were into church, and we both love God. On our journey, we were still getting to know one another, and in the process of getting to know one another, he asked me to marry him in 2013. I said yes even though we had only known each other a few months. At first, I thought it was too early. We both felt like the time was right and thought, Why wait when we know what we want? Well, we ended up going through a lot of things together. He was in between jobs, and he wasn't where he needed to be at the time, and that caused a lot of stress on our marriage. I was pulling all the weight by being the only one working and paying the bills. This happened over a timeframe of five of the six years of being married. I prayed every day for him. For us. After so long, I was tired. I prayed to God to give me guidance because by this time, I did not know what else to do. I was ready to give up, and one thing I promised myself was to never divorce. God gave me a dream within that same week that I was seeking guidance. In my dream, I remember being in a place that reminded me of home, and one of my close friends was with me, and I was going to her for advice in my marriage. My friend told me to go to the very root of where my ex-husband and I first met, and I would find the answer. I woke up, and the dream was still fresh on my mind. I started thinking about how he and I first met and how we established our relationship and marriage. It was then that I realized that we did not have a foundation. We didn't seek God for guidance, and we made moves on our own without seeking Him first.

My ex came to me and told me that he was not ready for marriage when we got married. He said that mentally he had not been in a place to get married. But he did it anyway because he wanted to be with me. I carried that around for a few weeks, and I prayed and asked God to show me what I needed to do. God spoke to me and told me that in order for my ex to mature into the man He called him to be, I was going to have to let him go. I told my ex that I prayed, and this was what God gave me. This was not an easy decision to make, but out of obedience, I let go. I filed for divorce in 2019. I told him that this was out of obedience more than anything, and we ended things in a peaceful manner. It took me a year to finally make that decision. I was ashamed at first because I was wondering if people would look at me differently and thought maybe my family or his family would look at me as a failure in my marriage. But God revealed to me that the decision was going to help me grow and help me get closer to Him. This decision allowed me to let go and let God have His way in my life. I heard from God more and more, and my relationship with Him grew. I learned things about myself that I never knew before. My focus was on God, and I did not allow anything or anyone to distract me. I was just like Peter in the Bible when it was storming and all chaos was breaking loose. In that story, everyone is distracted, and then God calms the storm and tells Peter to walk on water. In an act of faith, Peter stepped out of the boat, and he started walking on the water. He didn't realize what was going on right away. He was distracted and couldn't believe he was walking on the water. Then, he started to sink because he took his eyes off of God. For a moment, he lost focus.

Sometimes, all God wants us to do is trust Him. He wants us to trust that we can step out in faith outside of the boat. He wants us to know that as long we keep our eyes fixed on Him, we will stay afloat. It's only when we lose focus that we begin to sink. Our Purpose is to seek Him with all that we have, even the broken pieces of ourselves, and trust that God is going to put those pieces back together again. He is our Father, Healer of broken hearts and Mender of broken pieces. He is our refuge and our safe haven. Don't be afraid. Trust God!

Who Am I?

In November 2019, I went through the divorce, and I was learning to love myself a little stronger and learning not to be so hard on myself. I stayed in the face of God. Before 2019 ended, God spoke to me and told me that 2020 would be the year of perfect vision. He told me to keep my eyes focused on Him at all times and to not be distracted by what was going on in my environment. Well, in 2020, the COVID pandemic happened, and my faith was tested. I had anxiety all the time, and as a now-single mother of three children, I was afraid, but I had to remember what God said. At the time, God told me to keep my eyes focused on Him. I did not know why, but I trusted Him. He revealed to me that I had to be steadfast in the face of adversity and to never give up.

By the end of 2020, God spoke to me again, and this time, He told me to lay it all at His feet. I had to lay my fears, my anxiety, doubts, and even relationships down. I had an issue with trying to do everything on my own and worrying about how I was going to get things done.

God said, "Not this time."

God wanted me to surrender all, and I did. I had to let it go and give it to God. The moment I learned to give it to Him, He in return gave me peace. When I tell you that was life-changing...I can honestly say I live my life worrying less. It's all in God's hands, and when He has it, I don't have to worry about a thing. I have had people tell me I'm nonchalant or I don't care. No, that isn't it. God showed me how to walk in perfect peace. He showed me how to give it all to Him. I don't think that I'm better than the next; instead, I simply obeyed my Father, and His gift to me in return has saved my life. I pray daily, I walk with God daily, and I put my full trust in Him.

I do not want you to confuse this with religion because this is far from religion. This is about having relationship with God. As long as I am in one accord with the Father, the Son, and the Holy Spirit, then I am not focused on religion. I'm not picking and choosing a religion, but what I am doing is choosing to be in relationship with God. That is what God wants. I lay down my life and picked up the cross and followed God, and it has been and will continue to work for me. God has never led me in the wrong direction nor has He left me, but He has been good to me. He has built me up and transformed my life. God not only brings the Word to me, but He brings it through me for the building up of His Kingdom.

The beautiful thing about all of this is that I want to share it all with you. I don't want to do this by myself. I want my brothers and sisters to experience love and relationship with God, as well.

I was going through a phase in life in which I was learning who I was and what I liked and what grabbed my interest. After being in a marriage for six years and then divorcing, I knew what it was that I wanted and how I wanted to be treated. I knew that I did want to eventually remarry, and this time I want it to last. I want it to be a marriage built on a foundation of God's love. Dating can be hard, especially when you are in the process of preparation. I only want what God has for me, and I don't want to mess that up by trying to do things my way. Not only do I have to look out for myself, but I have to also prepare myself to be a better person for my future spouse. In this waiting season of my life, God is preparing me for marriage again in the future. Before God can reveal to me the spouse that is for me, I have to be ready for Him. I can't expect God to bless me with a man of God when I'm not in position to receive him. However, I do know that the man that God has for me will make himself known, he will speak with purpose, he will want to pray with me, he will cover me in prayer, and most importantly, he will put God first. A man who puts God first is a man who will lead me and our family back to God. I am certain that God will provide confirmation in the next relationship that I'm in because I am allowing Him to guide me this time. Plus, He knows what's best.

"I am certain that God, who began the good work within you, will continue his work until it is finally finished on the day when Christ Jesus returns" (Philippians 1:6, NLT). You and I have work to do. From the beginning of time, God put in us everything that He was going to put in us. We are on assignment, and we have to learn to separate business from pleasure. This is Kingdom business, carried out for the purpose of building up God's people and being in one accord with God. God handpicked you to be the fruit that will produce other fruit. God is creating covenant connections, bringing you into community with others who have resources to do His business.

Your heart's posture matters when it's God's business. We cannot get so caught up in the world that we lose sight of God. Our minds have to stay on the task set out for us. It is also important for us not to get our assignment mixed up with having a relationship with someone. Don't confuse the two. God will draw people to you on Purpose to help those people. You are on assignment to help the next person get through trials in life just like you did. I used to wonder why people would be so drawn to me. I mean, I could run into a strange, and they would tell me they could see that I walked in a different light. Growing up, I always felt different from my peers and like I didn't fit in. Well, it wasn't until I was older that I knew I walked a different walk, a walk in the light. I would feel the pain of others, and sometimes I could look at a person and discern them. I was carrying the glory of God. No wonder people were drawn to me or they just felt comfortable sharing their life struggles with me. Some would even come to me and ask me to pray for them, and I would wonder, How does this person know that I pray?

Please don't misread me as trying to boast about myself. No, I'm just simply speaking from a place of experience in my life, and maybe you can relate. In realizing my walk was different, I had to learn to walk in a different stature. I couldn't hang out with just anybody. I couldn't just speak any kind of way. I had to stop trying to fit in just because I wanted to feel accepted by everyone. I had to stop dimming my light just to fit in with the crowd. The feeling of not fitting in was on Purpose. God was tugging at me, trying to get my attention, and here I was, trying to force myself to be something that I wasn't.

Distractions are real. I had to have a one-on-one with myself and wake up to who I was in Christ. This wasn't an easy process; it was a daily battle. I would go back and forth repetitively. Sometimes, you have to pull yourself out of those places that feel familiar, or else you will be stuck in a place of stagnancy. Our Father in Heaven does not want us to be stagnant. He wants us to elevate so that we can see who we are. On this journey, you may lose a few peers along the way. Yes, I say "peers" because you may have thought they were your friends, and that is okay because what they say is irrelevant to you walking in your Purpose. But when God starts to elevate you to your higher calling, you will lose some friends along the way. Some will say you're acting different or you don't do the things you used to do. God will remove some things from you– and some people, too! God will stretch you and make you uncomfortable, and that is when you know it is a move from God.

Remove and Reveal

"See if there is any offensive way in me,
and lead me in the way everlasting."
Psalm 139:24 (NIV)

Prayer: "Heavenly Father, remove any ways of mine that are not Your ways. Remove any thoughts of mine that are not Your thoughts. Reveal to me Your truths and your ways so that I can live a righteous life, pleasing in Your eyes. In Jesus' name. Amen."

Praying this prayer not only allows you to get closer to God, but it reveals to you your ways. Sometimes, you have to move out of your own way and let God have His way. Let God reveal to you parts of yourself that you need to work on to become a better person– a better husband, a better wife, a better friend, or a better parent. Have you ever offended someone and in the moment, you didn't realize it until they brought it to your attention? I'm sure we have all at some point been there. Sometimes, our words and actions may offend someone, especially if they take it the wrong way. Words have power and have the tendency to manifest. I believe that is why our words can offend people. When we speak certain words, people feel them. I had to ask God to change my language so that I would speak out of love. "Create in me a clean heart...and renew a right spirit within me" (Psalm 51:10). Your heart's posture matters when it comes to any relationship in your life, whether it's at work, home, school, or church. The way you speak and the way you respond are important. Asking God to change some things about yourself requires you to be receptive to Him. Your heart has to be in position to receive God's best for you or unconsciously you will reject what He is doing inside of you. This will cause you to have a hardened heart. Have you ever heard of a hardened heart?

Well, any time a person is in a position where they don't receive anything spiritually, their heart is hardened. I want my heart to always be receptive because I don't want to miss out on what God is doing in my life. I don't want to be in a position where I'm seeking out God and I feel like I'm far away. If I feel like I can't hear from God, that's when I need to check my heart's posture. God does not want us out here lost or far away from His good grace. The will of God will never lead you where the grace of God cannot keep you. His will for you is to experience Heaven on Earth. You don't have to wait until you die to experience Heaven. Get closer to God and receive the good life that He has set out for you. Every day won't be a piece of cake. Some days will be better than others. But the goal is to persevere, no matter what we go through. God never said that it was going to be easy. God never said that we won't have trials and tribulations. We will– and yes, they do exist. Be of good cheer; God has overcome the world and deprived it of its power to harm you (John 16:33). This scripture helps me rest in His arms, knowing that I am safe with God and that, yes, I may have trials and tribulations, but I can find peace in knowing that God is with me. God is not going to allow His children to go through things without joy being on the other side. We must trust Him with our whole hearts. There will be things that come up against us all the time, and we must have peace of mind because He is our Protector. You walk in the grace of God daily. God woke you up this morning with Purpose. He started you on your destination today with Purpose. He will continue to lead you in Purpose. Your Purpose will cause you to elevate to a higher calling. When you begin walking in your Purpose, you may lose some along the way. God will reveal to you the hearts of the people in your life who are for you and the people who mean you no good. Some people are only in contact with you for the things that they can obtain from you. Beware of these people. You need genuine people in your life who don't want you to fail and who won't let you do things that will harm you. Anyone who will watch you walk right into the road of destruction is not a friend. God will remove and reveal the right people necessary for your growth in Him in your life. Walking in your Purpose will require you to be healed. The healing process can only begin to take place when you are ready to walk on that path. Some of us aren't ready, and it's not that we don't want to be healed, but there may be past traumas that we have to face. Healing starts when you go back to the root of that trauma, past hurt, or crisis that caused the brokenness in the first place. Whenever you face the things that caused you pain, you have to approach it knowing who you are in Christ. You are sons and daughters of Christ, and He wants us all to walk in freedom from bondage. If you are still carrying around past traumas, hurt, and pain, then you need to ask God to break you free from that bondage so that you can walk in freedom.

A prayer that you can pray to ask God to free you from bondage is:

"Heavenly Father, I come to You first giving You thanks for being who You are and allowing me to be reminded of who I am in You. I am Your child, and I want to walk in freedom. Fear will no longer hold me bound, doubt will no longer hold me down, brokenness will no longer hold me down, childhood traumas will no longer hold me down, and grief will no longer hold me down. I will from this day forward walk in healing because healing belongs to me. I am free, and I am whole, and no weapon formed against me will prosper. It will not work. In Jesus' name. Amen."

If you have to say this prayer daily, then do so. Pray until you see the change, and I will be praying that whoever prays this prayer will be set free from the bondage of pain. Our Purpose on this Earth is to be here for one another and help one another on this journey called life. We have to be willing to lift each other up and encourage one another because there is already enough pain and suffering going on today. We have to want to *be* the change in order to *see* the change. You are purposed for healing! I am my brothers' and sisters' keeper, and I am willing to do what it takes to save the next person. I don't want to win alone. I want to reach my hand out and bring up my brothers and sisters so they can walk in Purpose. You have what it takes to be purposeful and to have all that God created you to have. There are no limits to what God has for us. We mess up when we put a limit on God. God is not selfish, and He did not create us to be selfish, either. Scripture says, "For God so loved the world that he gave his only begotten son..." (John 3:16, NKJV). God performed an act of selflessness. He did that for you, and He did it for me and everyone else in this world. How dare we walk around being selfish? I'm not pointing fingers because I have been there, too. God did what He did on Purpose so that we would walk in salvation, so that we could be set free from bondage and walk in our calling. You are a child of God, created in His likeness to do the work in the Earth for His Kingdom. We are here on assignment for the Kingdom of God.

Chapter 4

†

Time, Patience, Perseverance

Never be in a rush because God's timing is perfect timing. God knows exactly what He is doing, so we don't have to feel like we have to hurry up to do a thing.

Ecclesiastes 3:1-8 says, "To everything there is a season, and a time to every purpose under the heaven...A time to get, and a time to lose; a time to keep, and a time to cast away; A time to rend, and a time to sew; a time to keep silence, and a time to speak; A time to love, and a time to hate; a time of war, and a time of peace."

There is a time and season for every walk of life. You may very well be in a season right now. Do not neglect the season of growth. Instead, trust the process. In due time, you will reap what you sow. Be patient in waiting because in the time of difficulty, God will give you the strength to persevere through any situation. Have you ever been in a season of stagnancy where nothing in your life was moving and it felt like you were at a standstill? There was no one to call on because you did not want to feel like you were bothering others. Or maybe you were in a situation where you had to make a decision that was too hard to make and you felt like you did not have the time you needed to think about it. What I have learned in life (and I am sure you have, too) is that time waits for no one. Most of the time, when you feel like nothing is moving in your life is the time when you need to get into the presence of God. If you need to turn on music, do that. Some people have prayer closets, and they find them as a source of peace. Whatever you must do, create the time and space for one-on-one time with God. The presence of God brings peace, and it sheds light on any situation. There is no better time than now to do what you're purposed to do. Therefore, make the time to pray and ask God to guide you on the path that He has for you. Your Purpose is waiting to be revealed. Someone can heal from your Purpose, and some may even be set free from bondage. You never know what impact you may have on the lives of others if you don't make the time for your Purpose. Time is of the essence, and what's on the inside of you is ready to be free!

Patience is a Virtue

When it comes to finding your Purpose, you have to adopt patience. Patience is the key to a successful and healthier mindset. When I get excited about my Purpose, I tend to be in a hurry, and I want it to manifest quickly. I must be reminded that with Purpose comes patience. There were times when I had to humble myself in some situations because I wanted to see things happen immediately. When we get in a rush, we may miss a thing or two because our minds are on the finished results. Being patient allows things to take their course, and slowly and surely the right things will fall into place.

Patience in the process will allow your Purpose to line up with the Word of God and the plans that He has for you to prosper. Be very aware that in waiting on the revelation of your Purpose, fear may try to creep in, anxiety may come and knock at your door, and doubt may come to try to steal your joy. Although these things may try to show up, you have to put on the full armor of God and set your mind and your desires on God. Lay it all at His feet. Yes, these distractions and more may come your way, and you may want to give up on patience. But you have to be steadfast, unmovable, and unshakeable. Stand your ground and don't allow things to cause you to get off the path to your success!

Patience builds perseverance. You will persevere through anything that comes up against you. You may not understand or even see it yet, but you are courageous, and you can do anything you put your faith into. What is faith? "Now faith is the substance of things hoped for, the evidence of things not seen" (Hebrews 11:1). You need to build your faith, and any time you get ready to build, you have to start with a foundation. That is why God wants us to be built up in the Word so that with anything that tries to come our way, we will have a sturdy foundation followed by a strong house that is ready at all times to take on opposition.

How do you build your faith? Building your faith starts by trusting God. Similar to you getting in your car every day with the expectation that your car will start when you put the key in the ignition, followed by the expectation that the car will take you from point A to point B. The same way you put your trust in your vehicle doing what you need it to do, you have to apply the same principle as it relates to trusting God. When it comes to trusting God, you have to do it wholeheartedly with a made up mind. I trust God. He is the head of my life, and I know without a doubt that He will never lead me into destruction. Instead, He will lead me on the path to righteousness. He is my Father, the One who woke me up this morning. He put breath in my body, and He gave me the desires of my heart. I really cannot imagine my life without Him; He has shown up and continues to show up in my life daily.

In the Bible, Abraham was a man of faith. God called Abraham the father of many nations. God also told Abraham that his wife Sarah, who was ninety years old, would have a baby. Can you imagine a baby being born to a ninety-year-old couple? Well, three men visited Abraham and told him that his wife was going to have a baby. Sarah overheard the conversation and laughed to herself. She didn't believe that she was going to have a baby at an old age. Abraham believed, and because of his faith, she got pregnant and gave birth to a son. Faith is a touchpoint to receive from God. It was by Abraham's faith that he and his wife had a baby at an old age. Faith will cause the impossible to be possible. Believe without any doubts and trust God by standing firm in Him. Faith without works is dead. You have to put in the work and believe by simply choosing to trust God. Whatever may be causing you to worry, you have to know that God is already behind the scenes working things out in your favor. Have you ever been praying about something or even worried about something and things turned out to work in your favor? That is similar to how faith works. God is already working it out for you. Just continue to trust in Him. "God is not a man, that He should lie, Nor a son of man, that he should repent" (Numbers 23:19).

Lay it All at His Feet

No matter what you are doing, no matter where you are, and no matter what you're facing, God wants you to lay it all at His feet. Go to God with all that you have– your pain, disappointments, abandonment, betrayal, lies, backstabbing, and backsliding. God wants every piece of you. In return, He will give you peace of mind. Matthew 11:28-30 says, "Then Jesus said, 'Come to me, all you who are weary and burdened, and I will give you rest. Take my yoke upon you and learn from me, for I am gentle and humble in heart..."

I remember asking God to use me as a vessel. I want to lead people back to God and be an example for God. So many people are hurting and lost. They don't know who to turn to and who will listen. I found my greatest friend in God. I just want to help someone else find Him, too. He is very near to us all. All we have to do is draw close to God, and He will draw even closer to us. One thing I know is that God will never lead you into the wilderness or into a place where you feel lost, but He will set the path for you to get through it. Try to remember while you are on the path to trust the process.

Chapter 5

†

Enlarge Your Territory

"Jabez cried out to the God of Israel, 'Oh, that you would bless me and enlarge my territory! Let your hand be with me, and keep me from harm so that I will be free from pain. And God granted his request."
1 Chronicles 4:10 (NIV)

God will and wants to enlarge your territory! He will put you in a position to make room for the things that He has for you. When God elevates you, your gifts will go out and bless others and cause them to increase as well. This is overflow and abundance. I am not talking about earthly things like a big house or a nice car. I am talking about the fruit in you that will go out and produce other fruit. Allow God to use you in a way that others see your heart for what it really is. People will respect you for the light of God they see on you and in your life. Never be afraid of letting your light shine; the influence you have on others may help them to begin to walk in their Purpose, as well. The moment you start seeing other people around you elevate is the moment you will realize that what you are doing is causing a positive impact on the lives of the people around you. A lot of the time, people get so messed up because they see people mimicking their behavior. We have to get away from that because this isn't about being greedy and having it all for ourselves, but instead this is about helping our brother or sister out. I want everyone around me to win and more. God didn't give us gifts for us to keep them to ourselves. He wants us to share so that the next person can come up, as well. Let's be mindful, bring each other up, encourage each other, and also be mentors or friends to others trying to get somewhere in life. Life is already a battle as it is. We have so much going on, like this pandemic, the stress of life, the stress on family, and work. No one wants to feel like they are being a bother to others, so we have to love one another genuinely and operate out of the spirit of love.

One lesson I learned is that you cannot force God on anyone; they have to want God for themselves. I used to want everyone to know God and experience God, and I would tell them how He has been in my life. But for some reason, some people (even some close family members) could really not care less for what I was saying. I would even invite family and friends to church. Some would show up once and never come again, and some never showed up at all. Yes, I would get in my feelings about it because all I wanted was for them to experience God in their lives like I was. Well, that quickly changed one day when I reached out to my great grandmother, a wonderful woman of God. God rest her soul. On that day when I called, I was letting her know how it bothered me that some of my close family and friends didn't want to join me and go to church.

She said in her calm voice, "You can't force God on people. They have to want God on their own, and when they are ready, they will go to God."

She was so right. I couldn't expect people to be hungry for God like I was. But what I could do was tell them about the goodness of the Lord and how He showed up in my life and changed my life. No, I'm not perfect. I was once lost in my way, too, and the beauty of it all is that I'm still learning and growing on my walk with God. One thing I don't do is look at people differently for not wanting to experience God. Instead, I love them, and I show them the same love that God shows me. Doing this makes me want to get closer to God because you never know who is watching and you never know who God will send into your life for you to help. The scripture says, "With love and kindness have I drawn them" (Jeremiah 31:3), and it is so! The love and kindness that God gives to me draws me closer to Him, and it makes me want to dig deeper so that I can strengthen my relationship with Him. I don't want to be like the world. I want to be more like God. So, I read my Bible. I study the Word. Daily, I have to apply myself because I want to help other people get closer to God and experience Him, as well. It's just like sharing the good things that come your way because you want other people to have the same things you have. If someone teaches me how to gain wealth, then I can teach someone else, and then we all can get it. In the same way, God is giving me wisdom. I want to share this wisdom. I don't want to keep it all to myself. Proverbs 4:7 says, "Wisdom is the principle thing." With wisdom come understanding and the opportunity to gain wealth. As I have stated before, we are put here to help each other, not to compete. If there is anything in this world that I could be doing to help someone, it would be helping them pursue their Purpose.

You are bigger than you think, and when you begin seeking God, He will back you up every step of the way. The gifts from God are irrevocable, and He wants you to use what He put in you. You have what it takes to be the best version of yourself while sharing what is on the inside of you. You never know who is watching and learning from you.

I was at work one day, and this young lady stopped me and said, "Hey, I just wanted to let you know that every day I come into work, I look forward to seeing you because you always seem to have a smile on your face, and that alone gives me joy and peace when I come to work."

All I could do was smile because I had decided to choose joy every day and walk in it, and it was causing someone else to have it, too! The lives we live should cause a domino effect. Someone could be learning to be a better person from just watching you. Your words of affirmations may be helping someone who is close to giving up. No matter what you do, don't neglect your gifts even if they are small because a million little things equal up to the one big thing that may change someone else's life. Remember that you have a smile that can light up a room full of people. The presence of God that is on you will cause people to notice you, and you won't even have to do much to be seen. It's simply in your stature, the way you walk, the way you talk, and the way you pay attention to someone when they are speaking. God is making room for you and expanding your territory. He is simply allowing you to be recognized so that when the time comes you will have built a platform that will make room for your Purpose.

God Will Give You Provision

Trust God. He knows what He is doing, and He will give you wisdom, insight, and direction. No matter where you go or how far you go, God is never too far away to get you a word or a blessing. I remember I was getting ready to enroll back into college, and I was going back and forth with the decision to start or to wait. I didn't think that I would be able to go to school, be a mom, work, and focus. I was at church, and this lady who didn't even know my situation approached me and told me that she was led to tell me to "trust the process". I went with that, and that following week, I went and enrolled in classes. While I was waiting to speak to the advisor about my classes, I noticed on the white board at her desk a sign that read, "Trust the Process". To me, that was all the confirmation that I needed to show me that I would be successful in my endeavors. I passed that semester.

I'm currently in school while writing my first book, and I am still trusting the process. That lesson taught me that there is nothing that I cannot do! God wants us to trust Him. He wants us to have faith in knowing we are not alone. In fact, He walks with us every day. Whatever it is that God is showing you and whatever it is that you are having second thoughts about, I want to encourage you to trust God.

Proverbs 3:5-6 (NKJV) says, "Trust in the Lord with all your heart, and lean not on your own understanding; In all your ways acknowledge him, and he shall direct your paths."

If we were to try to do things without God, we would mess things up. I used to wonder why things did not work out in my favor when I was trying to do things my way. I was quickly reminded that without God, I am nothing. I need Him in all that I do. I am not trying to force God on anyone. I just want to challenge you to try God. God is our source, and everything else in our lives is a resource. Those resources are simply products of what God has already created for our lives to function. For example, our jobs, stores, food, cars, and so on are resources, and God is the primary source of those things. When God created you, He already had in mind the things that He wanted you to do. If only we could see ourselves the way that God sees us. The value and worth that He sees in us would blow our minds.

I honestly think that I would cry tears of joy for days if I could see myself through God's eyes. God loves every single one of us. He created every strand of hair on our heads and everything down to the soles of our feet, and He wants the best for us, so why not walk in Purpose? We are all His beloved children, and we shall have what He says we shall have. God wants us to be happy. He wants us to live in abundance. He wants us following and living out the desires of our hearts.

Chapter 6

†

Distractions Come To Sidetrack You

On the journey to your Purpose, there will be bumps in the road that try to distract you and get you off the course that God has set for you. Remember that you are destined for greatness and that you have what it takes no matter what. Every single step that you take, God will be right there leading you, right where you need to be. Those moments when you begin to see distractions are when you need to draw back closer to God. I have experienced moments in my life when distractions have come, and I had to be careful because distractions came from work, kids, family, friends, the news, and even myself. I had to carve out time from my schedule and make it a point to pray and seek God so that I could focus. I also had to remember that I had work to do, and I couldn't allow distractions to get me off course. I had to remember that it was significant for me to do the work God has called me to do because at the end of the day, this isn't about me. It's about leading people toward their Purpose and helping people pick up the broken pieces in their lives and taking them back to God where they can find healing. God is bigger than any circumstance in your life that tries to rise above your Purpose. The spirit of God resides in you, and that is why you feel the tug pulling you closer to God. That is why you can't allow those thoughts of what others may think of you take you off the course that He has set out for you. The moment you begin to face those distractions and put your full focus on God is the moment you will begin lining up with what the Word of God has for you. God will align His Word to your calling, and you will start seeing doors open on your behalf, signs and wonders taking place, and healings manifest before your eyes. I'm not telling you something that I read in a magazine. I am speaking from the places in my life where God showed me the same things. This is why it is vital for our works to be done with our minds made up to do His will, knowing that adversity will come and believing that we will overcome it by the grace of God.

God said in His Word that we will live life more abundantly. Therefore, if I lack in any area of my life, then I need to align that area with what the Word of God says concerning my life. Any person, place, or thing that causes me to feel empty, or if I'm lacking in area of my life, then I need to evaluate. The Word of God is a river of living water. I shall thirst no more, which means He is all I need, and I don't have to go to any other source.

In those moments when you feel like you are lost and you don't know where to start, begin by seeking God. God will in return give you wisdom, which is the key principle to understanding what it is that He wants you to do. When God gives you understanding and you start reading the words in the Bible, they will begin to make more sense to you. After you get understanding, God will begin to counsel you and give you insight into your Purpose, which will lead you right into the hands of fortitude. Fortitude will give you courage to take on anything that tries to come your way to distract you, and you will stand your ground because of the strength on the inside of you. This will cause you to draw closer to God because you will be hungry for His presence and His purpose for you. I encourage you to draw closer to God and not to neglect the moment of intimacy with

God. God will pour into you and fill your cup until it overflows, and when it overflows, you will have plenty to share with those around you.

Chapter 7

†

He Set You Up For A Time Like This

This is a setup! Your Purpose is a setup, waiting on you to answer it so that you can fulfill your destiny. It's the same as when He set the stars in the sky so that they would be light in the darkness, the same as when He set the firmament in the sky to separate Heaven and Earth. Everything under the sun has a purpose, and so do you. When you recognize what your Purpose is, you can't be afraid, although it may look bigger than you or it may seem impossible to you. You have to get up every day and chase your dreams or someone else will.

You are extraordinary, and you have what it takes to be who He created you to be. Your destination was already mapped out the moment you were conceived. Your path is paved with victory! Your Purpose and calling will set you free!

When God elevates you to walk in Purpose, you must know that someone is depending on you for healing, for the breaking of bondage, and for transformation, so you don't have time to waste. This may be your season to accelerate because there is a young lady who needs to hear your testimony so that she can find hope. There may be a young man who is struggling daily with his identity, and because you decided to be obedient and answer the call to Purpose, he will finally see himself in Christ. Don't neglect the process just because things aren't moving at the speed that you are expecting them to move. This goes back to that "microwave" lifestyle that we so easily want to lean towards because we want things to happen now, which will only cause things to happen in our lives prematurely. When a woman is pregnant, she must carry the baby for nine months. If the baby is born before those nine months, then the baby will be premature. Then, the baby may need to be in the hospital a little while until they reach a mature level before they are released. Similarly, if we rush what God is trying to do in our lives, we cause things to happen out of order. God is a God of order, and we have to take things one day at a time while realizing that each day is a day to work towards our Purpose. Each day is a day that someone can be set up to walk in freedom. The calling on your life is necessary because someone else's needs to be set free from bondage. I don't mean to sound harsh, but this assignment is not about you, and you have to get out of the selfish mindset. You have to be willing to lay down your life so that the next person can be set free. Your sister is depending on you. Your sons and daughters need you so that they can see what walking in Purpose looks like. You have the tools to do the work and fulfill your vision, and you have God backing you up to make sure you fulfill your destiny. Reach for the stars above you. Yes, they may seem far off, but the more faith you have in touching them, the more you will believe in yourself to never give up. I have been feeling this tug from God for some time now. But guess what I did – I procrastinated, I let fear get in the way, I let doubt get in the way, I let the thought of what others may think and say get in the way. When I look back over my life, I am reminded of all the times that God was there for me and how He never gave up on me. His Word says that He will never leave me nor forsake me. His Word is His truth, and God is not a man that He should lie. So, I can't give up,

I can't give in. I will go forward and push until I complete the task. You have to give it all that you've got because God has chosen you to do so.

Chapter 8

†

Dreams, Visions, Goals

I'm convinced that we all have dreams that we want to see manifested. We have visions of someday being in a place in life where we may not be at the moment. We all have goals that we want to meet. The beautiful thing about it all is that you have what it takes, my friend. You are an innovator, and God has given you the power to call those things out that you want to see, but you have to believe in it more than anything. You want to start the business? Then put a prayer on it, and God will give you the plan. I started writing in my journal in 2019, and at first, I did not have a book in mind. In fact, I was just writing down the dreams that God was revealing to me. I would write down goals that I wanted to accomplish and put dates on visions I wanted to see manifested. I also found myself writing down scriptures that encouraged me and affirmations that would help me make it through my day. Some days, I would get off work, do my daily "mom" routine, and then get some time to myself and just write. Some days, I felt like I was just writing to God, talking to Him about how I felt about things in my life and ways that I wanted to be a better person. My favorite part about writing in my journal was that I would have these moments when I would write down my prayers and declarations, and then I would go back and read them and reflect over how they happened in my life. Writing in my journal also gave me a sense of peace and joy because it would take me to a place mentally where I felt like God's presence was with me. Have you ever felt the spirit of God in your space? Well, let me tell you, I can't fully explain how it feels, but it's a feeling that I want everyone I know and more to experience. It's a feeling of wholeness and healing. It makes you feel supernatural, and it drives you to want to become your best self. I'm here to tell you that you can experience the presence of God, too. He is never too far away from you.

One of my favorite prayers to pray is the Lord's prayer. In fact, I learned this prayer when I was nine years old. I would say this prayer every night before bed, and I had it memorized. It's Matthew 6:9-13.

I would say:

"Our Father which art in Heaven, Hallowed be thy name. Thy kingdom come, thy will be done in earth, as it is in Heaven. Give us this day our daily bread. And forgive us our trespasses, as we forgive those who trespass against us. And lead us not into temptation, but deliver us from evil; For yours is the kingdom, and the power, and the glory, forever and ever. In Jesus' name. Amen."

Saying this prayer as a child made me feel safe, but as an adult, I was enlightened because it brought me peace, and I also wanted to seek God more to do His will. I wanted to be used by God to help people by being an influence. I had to get my life together. I had to be honest with myself because how could I influence others if I wasn't living for God? No, I don't believe that I am perfect, nor do I believe that everything I do in my life is right. But what I do believe is that every day I can push towards the mark of being a better person and a better friend and being someone who is willing to uplift and inspire the next. I want to encourage you to fulfill your vision. I want you to chase your dreams, I want you to accomplish your goals. There are going to be days where you want to give up, where you don't feel like your best, and that is okay. What you don't accomplish today, God will give you the next day to start again. You are more than a conqueror through Christ Jesus. Tap into your God-given power and find the strength that He put inside of you. Keep being great because you are amazing and you have exactly what it takes. There is not one person on this Earth who has what you have. You are different from the rest, you stand out, you make a difference, and you have life-changing capabilities. You are someone's hope, and you have something for the generations to come. You are a dreamer who has what it takes to accomplish the vision that God has given you, and you will tackle your goals with the ambition that's on the inside of you. Seek God, and He will reveal your heart's desires to you. I had no idea I was going to be writing a book. Five years ago, I would have never thought of seeing myself as an upcoming author. What I do know is that I was created for this. God purposed me for this. God gave me the vision, and He told me to write it down. He showed me the dream and put it in my heart to help others. I am not doing this for me, nor am I doing this for the likes of man. What I am doing is purposeful. I want God to get the glory and all of the shine. God is simply using me as a vessel, and if I had decided to ignore this or if I chosen not to do what I'm doing, then what good would that serve? God created us as masterpieces, created to live out our Purpose in this world. I don't want to sit around knowing that there is something that I can be doing to serve others. You are purposed for greatness, and don't let a soul tell you what you cannot do, not even yourself.

I dare you to look in the mirror and say, "Hello, dreamer! Hello, goal-crusher! Hello, visionary!"

Whoever it is that you see yourself as, start speaking and showing up as that person. You are remarkable. Therefore, when you walk in the room, the whole atmosphere changes because God is walking with you and He is causing your light to influence others. People are going to start approaching you, asking you what it is that you are doing differently. They will tell you that you are glowing. They will want to know what it is that they need to do to start living the same way as you. Walking in Purpose is a lifestyle. It is a decision that you make based on the positive light that you want to shed on others. You may not know what you need to be doing or what you want to be doing right now, but I promise you that God can and will reveal that to you. The moment you stop seeking the platform and you start seeking your Purpose, God will make room for your Purpose to start manifesting. I encourage you not to get in the way of what God is doing in your life by trying to take the spotlight. Instead, be humble and allow God to take the wheel and lead you. Your Purpose is a passion that is pulling and tugging at you to get done. You will know this because it will come to your mind every day and you will feel bad if you don't start working at it daily. You cannot allow the light that God gives you to go out. In fact, I'm here to tell you that there will be days when that light starts to dim down, but don't let it get to the point where it no longer burns.

You don't want your light to go out. You want your light to cause a positive effect on the lives of the people around you. God will put you exactly where you are supposed to be at the most opportune moments in your life. You will know this because everything in your life will align with the Word of God. Strangers will respect you, and they will want to get close to you because they will feel the glory that is on you. This may all seem overwhelming, but you have to remember to keep your mind set on God. God is elevating you, and with elevation, there comes separation. You have to separate yourself from feelings of fame. God is exposing you to people and setting you up to become His full-time servant. This is a higher lifestyle that will cause you to have to adhere to a certain standard, and you can't mix old with new. What I am saying is you cannot live life for God and also want to hold on to your old self. You are growing, and with growth comes change. Therefore, you have to keep your eyes on God daily. If you have to, start each day with a prayer so that it sets the tone for that day. When I get up in the morning, I decree how my day will go. Yes, obstacles may come, but that's when you remind them of what God says.

My declarations would go like this:

"Lord, I thank You that today will be a good day, a productive day, and although obstacles may come my way, I will be reminded that You said in Your Word that no weapon formed against me shall prosper, and I will do whatever it is that You would have me to do today. Amen."

Some days, I may say something different. It all depends on where the Holy Spirit is leading me. You may not be in control of what happens to you throughout your day, but you are in control of how you respond. There was a time when I had to check myself daily. I couldn't allow people or situations to take me out of my element. I had to pray and ask God to not only change my language but also change my reaction, as well. I wanted the words that came out of my mouth to speak life and blessings, not death and curses.

This wasn't an overnight process. This took time and this took repentance. Just like the scripture says in Psalm 19:14, "Let the words of my mouth, and the meditation of my heart, be acceptable in thy sight, O Lord, my strength, and my redeemer." I had to rely on the strength of God to keep me (and my mouth) some days. Adversity can be our biggest opposition, and I didn't want to say words that would hurt others, nor did I want to say things that would make my situation worse. I had to learn to speak from a place of love, and I'd ask myself, "What is the best way to respond to this?" I noticed that when I took my time and thought about what I was going to say or how I was going to approach the situation, my response was not negative. In fact, it caused a positive reaction. Then, I would look back over the times when I would have responded quickly and out of anger and realize that usually made things worse. It always matters how we respond; our response determines the reaction. I pray that you begin seeking God from this day forward when it comes to speaking life to your situation so you will have what you say you will and so God can lead you to a lifestyle full of Purpose and dreams and goals that will set you up to becoming all that He has created you to be.

Moments of Revelation

There are going to be times when God says, "Go!" When you hear the voice of God telling you to make a move, you have got to be ready to make that move. You can't second-guess it, and you can't be worried about what the next person will say. You have to know and trust that God is leading the way. When God first spoke to me about this book assignment, I'm going to be honest with you, I did not have confidence in it. I was afraid, and I procrastinated because I did not think it was going to reach people. God said, "Do it, anyway, and trust that I will create the path for you." People are hurting, people are lost, people need God, and God wants you to lead them to Him. The people who are hurting need to heal. The people who are lost need guidance. God did not put the answers inside of me. Instead, He gave me the wisdom to draw closer to Him so that He could instruct me with wise counsel. I'm not doing this for my own benefit. I'm doing this for my mother, my father, my sister, my brother, my children, my children's children, and the generations to come. This assignment is beyond me, and God had to build me up so that I could be ready to do His works. I spent time in the face of God for wisdom and for instruction so that I could be pure in heart and in the right mindset. I had to let go of some people in my life whom I thought I needed. I had to stop hanging around certain people. I had to let go of conversations that did not serve a purpose. I had to stop pretending to be someone I wasn't. I had to find out who I was, the real deal, because the life that God was calling me to was drawing me closer. God was calling me to be His workmanship, to prophesy to His people, and to let them know His plans. I pray that God will reveal to you your Purpose in Him and that you won't be confused because you will know when He is speaking to you. God will do what He has to do to get your attention, so always be attentive and incline your ear to hear Him. Get in His Word for understanding. Try God because scripture says in Matthew 11:30 that His work is easy and His burden is light. God wants the very best for us as His children. He wants us to rise above our old selves and begin walking in newness.

I know that you like new things, new clothes, new shoes, a new house, a new car. What about a new you? God makes all things new, including you if you let Him. God will give you a glimpse of what "good" looks like so that He can grab your attention. You don't have to wait until you get to Heaven to experience God's best. God is ready for you to surrender, to fully come to Him with a mindset to do His will, and to stop allowing the opinions and views of other people hinder you from experiencing God's goodness.

God created you on Purpose to do His will. You have everything inside of you at this moment that you are supposed to have. God is not waiting on you so that He can put things in you. He put everything inside of you in the beginning while He was creating this world. God sent His son Jesus to the Earth on Purpose to save our lives and set us up for our Purpose and destiny. When Jesus went through betrayal, it was on Purpose. When He was beaten, it was on Purpose. He had work to do, and He knew His Purpose. The devil tried to tempt Jesus, and He didn't let him take Him off the path for His Purpose. Jesus had His mind set on what it was that He was sent to do. All the way up until they hung Jesus on the cross, He still had Purpose on His mind. He died on Purpose so that you and I could live. He even asked God to forgive the people who wronged Him. God set you up to do great works through Jesus Christ.

John 14:12 says, "...He that believeth on me, the works that I do shall he do also; and greater works than these shall he do; because I go unto my Father."

You were created to do great things on the Earth for the building up of God's Kingdom. You have the power to thrive and to elevate your mind to your higher calling.

God chose you to influence and lead, and the time is now. The longer you wait to walk in Purpose, the longer the person waiting to receive their breakthrough will have to wait, too. You may not see your Purpose right now, you may not feel your Purpose, and you may not even look like your Purpose. But God is setting you up for Purpose, and I want to stand in agreement with you so that you will begin to see and fulfill your Purpose. I had to make my mind up to get up every day and seek my Purpose because God did not create me to be mediocre. He created me to be extraordinary. That is why I cannot give up. That is why the late nights and early mornings will all makes sense. When you are pregnant with Purpose, there will be days when you find yourself getting ready for what is to come. When a woman is pregnant, she will have growing pains, she will be up late because she's uncomfortable, and she will start gathering the things that she will need for the baby's arrival. Not only does she have to prepare physically, but she also has to prepare mentally for the life change that is about to take place. She has to get out of any selfish mindset because it will no longer be all about her; she will now have another person to think about. Whatever it is that you are destined to do, just know you have to get ready for all of it – the long hours it's going to take to get where you want to be, the lives of others that you will influence, and the elevation that God is about to help you reach.

I just want to know: are you ready to receive God's best?

I pray that you don't give up on your dreams. There will be days when you feel like giving up and you feel burned out, but I want to encourage you to lean on God for your strength. He started the good works in you, and He put the vision inside of you for you to finish it. God gave you the vision because He knew that He could trust you to carry it out to its fullness. Don't give it up now. You have come too far to turn back now.

If you ever feel like you can't make it, just know that God will carry you through the troubled waters. The first thing that you need to do is get rid of all distractions so that you can see and hear God. God will never allow you to walk alone on troubled waters because He is guiding, protecting, and reassuring you the whole way through. Don't give up now. Your breakthrough is right around the corner, so you have to hold on. Your testimony will be the blessing that will save so many people, so be steadfast.

Completeness: The Finished Work

You are the finished work, the manifestation, and the example of what it looks like because you chose to keep going instead of giving up. You chose to walk in Purpose even when it was hard to, and you had what it took to fight the good fight that led you to redemption. Your "yes" to God opened doors for you that you could have never imagined having access to. Your life will continue to transform because of your obedience to God, and your relationship with God will flourish as you begin to seek Him every day. The words that you speak will only be words that speak life because God has given you a new language. Therefore, you walk in holiness. The lives of the people who are connected to you will be full of abundance because you chose to follow God and walk in Purpose. You are no longer afraid to walk on this new journey with God because He is your source. No matter what, if you choose to walk alone, you won't ever feel alone because God is always with you.

Look at you! You made it through those moments when you thought you were going to give up. You kept pushing when things got tough, and when adversity came to knock you down, it failed because you were steadfast. From the beginning of time, you were purposed on Purpose for greater works, and there isn't a devil in hell that can stop you. Not now, not ever. You are the product of what it looks like to walk in glory. There were people along the way who doubted you. There were situations that came and tried to hold you bound. You trusted God, and you let Him lead you, encourage you, strengthen you, and align you with Purpose. You found out that the only person holding you back was you. But you are greater now. You walk taller now with your head held high because nothing can stop what God has ordained. The glory glow is upon your face, and everyone is attracted to your light. That's okay; don't take it the wrong way. Instead, use it to elevate yourself so that you can lead more people back to God. You will tell your story of how you almost gave up, how everyone counted you out, how no one believed in you and then God gave you beauty for ashes. Now everyone wants to know how you made it. They want to know what it is that they can do to get to where you are. The most graceful thing about it all is that you won't be like them. You won't turn your back on them because you are different, so you tell them how it was all God.

God called you to be complete in Him, and He is the head of all principality and power. Therefore, your job cannot complete you, your spouse cannot complete you, your kids cannot complete you, materialistic things will not complete you, and your relationship cannot complete you. Only God can complete you, and if you seek completeness from any other source, it will only be temporary and will lead you back to emptiness. It will cause you to always be in a cycle of repetitiveness, and you will be looking for ways to get out of it. You can help yourself by allowing God to order your steps. God is the Originator, and Jesus is the Mediator who is able to intercede on our behalf. So, allow God to have His way, and if He asks you to help your brother, do it. If He asks you to bless your sister, do it. Don't miss out on your blessing by refusing to be a blessing. You friend may need to see God through you so that they can begin to be healed and set free. Your family needs you to walk in your calling so that they can be led by example. Your Purpose is calling you to do the will of God so that someone in this world can be led to healing and walk in freedom. The next time you encounter someone, show them love. When you speak to people, speak out of love. Whenever you do any work, do it with love. God is love, and when He created you, He created you out of love.

"Let all that you do be done with love."
1 Corinthians 16:14 (NKJV)

Words of Affirmation

Lord, I rise early, and I seek You. First, I want to thank You for waking me up this morning. Thank You for protecting me to and from my destinations and for dispatching angels to watch over me as I go out on my journey. Thank You for the abundance of life and love that You allow to overflow in my life. Today will be a day that brings joy and laughter and a day of productivity in which I will lack nothing. Thank You for the things that You are doing for me and my family, both now and forevermore. In Jesus' name. Amen.

About the Author

Janice Buckley was born in Blytheville, Arkansas and currently lives in Jonesboro, Arkansas. She moved to Jonesboro in 2013 and has been employed at Frito-Lay for five years as an inventory specialist. Janice is a mother to three wonderful children: Jailon and Jaila are twins, age thirteen, and Martez Junior is five years old. Janice says, "For as long as I can remember, I have always loved God. I am a believer in God, and I believe He spoke to me in 2019 and told me to write, so here I am!"

Also Available from J. Kenkade Publishing

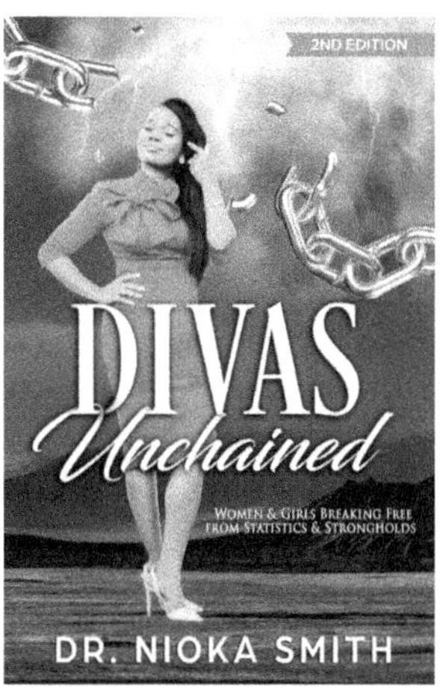

ISBN: 978-1-944486-25-9
Visit www.drniokasmith.com
Author: Dr. Nioka Smith

Sexually abused by her father at the age of 14, pregnant at the age of 17, and a nervous breakdown at the age of 28, Dr. Nioka Smith's painful past almost killed her, until the voice of the Lord guided her into destroying strongholds and reversing Satan's plan for her life. DIVAS Unchained is the powerful chain-breaking reality of the many unfortunate strongholds our women and girls face. Dr. Nioka uses her divine gift to help women and girls break free from destructive life cycles and prosper in all areas of life. Satan has lied to you. It's time to expose his lies. It's time to break free!

Also Available from J. Kenkade Publishing

ISBN: 978-1-944486-98-3
Visit www.amazon.com
Author: Trena Ford

"Just Breathe" is the true story of a small-town girl born in the Delta. The youngest girl of five children, Trena Ford's life was changed radically when her family relocated to follow an evangelical church ministry. Throughout her childhood and into her mature years, she had a special bond with her father that granted her opportunities to experience triumphs as well as heartbreaks. She tells the story of how a cancer diagnosis, devastation, and death uncovered an unshakeable seed of faith buried deep within her soul. Through pain and several medical procedures, she was given a formula that birthed new life into her desire to overcome cancer, live on purpose, and fulfill God's plan for what He created her to be.

Also Available from J. Kenkade Publishing

ISBN: 978-1-944486-83-9
Visit www.amazon.com
Author: Apostle C. A. Turner

There's such a hunger for the things of the spirit and the supernatural. Many have decided to tap into the dark side in order to understand more about the Supernatural and the things of the spirit. One of the reasons for this I believe, is because the church as a whole has lost the desire to see a move of God validated by his power with miracles, signs, and wonders. It's my desire and prayer that this information will activate you in ways you never dreamed as you apply it to your spiritual life.

Also Available from J. Kenkade Publishing

ISBN: 978-1-944486-72-3
Visit www.amazon.com
Author: Jerry Walker

Do you find yourself asking the question, "Is there more to life than the seemingly never-ending struggle of survival?" This book answers that question with a resounding, "YES!" Jesus died to give us MORE. Jerry Walker has written this manual for Christian living that gives in-depth teaching on scripture and how to apply it to your life. Full of tools for living a life of freedom in Christ, this book will be a blessing to all who read it. Your time is now, it truly is your season!

www.ingramcontent.com/pod-product-compliance
Lightning Source LLC
LaVergne TN
LVHW010106110826
845155LV00028B/514

* 9 7 8 1 9 5 5 1 8 6 0 3 2 *